Dedicated to my parents,
Barbara and Harold

TABLE OF CONTENTS

INTRODUCTION

Design is, by nature, a visual process. You look at site conditions, and at materials, colors, and textures. You keep an eye on size and proportion, and on light and views. All of these elements matter but none of them amount to much if an interior doesn't make you feel, well, good—through and through.

Think of the spaces where you have been happiest. You may be able to only vaguely describe the decorative elements of a room but the effect they had on your sense of delight and well-being will ring true and clear. Chances are the details you recall will not be the fireplace andirons or hearthside chair and ottoman, but the evocative scent of wood smoke and the perfect position of repose you were able to assume.

Something as simple as the way a room glowed, the sympathetic coming together of color and light, may be what stays with you. It's that sense of comfort, of being cared for and uplifted, that makes the biggest imprint and endows only certain places with lasting influence and special affection.

Some of my fondest memories are from the sleepovers I had on my maternal grandparents' Virginia farm in the foothills of the Blue Ridge Mountains. The farmhouse itself was like an illustration from a children's book: a friendly story-and-a-half white clapboard dwelling with a red tin hat. After a day of fishing and unloading hay bales and gathering eggs from the chicken coop, we tuckered-out kids climbed to a bedroom under the eaves. Nothing was so magical as being there during a summer storm, feeling warm and secure as the rain pitter-pattered or pounded down above us, its rhythms accentuated by the metal roof.

It's probably no accident that my house in Atlanta, also a nineteenth-century white clapboard building with long, low roof, strikes such a familiar chord. No matter how far we roam from where we grew up, it stays with us. Just as a regional accent can bubble to the surface, especially when talking to folks from home, visual references from earlier periods of our lives tiptoe into our adult environments.

I have lived in Atlanta all of my professional life but Virginia is the note that resonates in everything I do. The simple pleasures of farm life were one influence. Greens and blues and natural woods have always dominated my palette. My favorite neutral has long been a deep gray-brown, the color of bark and certain weathered wood. A textile I turn to again and again is antique Flemish tapestry, especially if it has an animal hiding in the stylized blue-green foliage. I can't help but think my attraction to such calm, natural hues reflects the peaceful, happy days I spent on my grandparents' farm and on my own parents' land with its pastures and panorama of rolling hills.

My maternal grandmother had a wonderful way of mixing periods and styles. Over the English camelback sofa hung a big mirror with a carved, gilded frame, its sparkly plane of silver a demonstration of how something so simple can have such an animating impact on a room. Between two chairs she placed a Korean chest, a souvenir of her travels, to serve as a table. It was the most exotic thing I had seen, and its display taught me the broad value of embracing the unfamiliar and the specific merit of adding a note of curiosity to an interior.

Her daughter, my mother, has had, not surprisingly, the greatest impact on the development of my style, in ways far more profound than surface or form. Not that she, a lover of porcelain, didn't teach me all about the makers' marks on the underside, or school me on the various forms of furniture. "Always examine the legs," she advised me, when assessing antique tables and chairs, "it's the feet that tell the story." My interiors are sometimes considered a bit masculine, probably because of their palette, but rare is the room I have not softened or even feminized via the curvaceous form of a cabriole leg.

Virginians are proud of their history, which runs as deep as the gentility of this most northern of the southern states. Graciousness is as much a part of our genetic makeup as directness is in a Yankee. At Monticello, Thomas Jefferson not only invited guests to dine in an elegant, interesting, and intimate house, he served them rare treats from his garden and fine wines from France. Moreover, he encouraged congenial, easy conversation at the table, rare for its time, the guidelines for discussion being "no health, no politics, no restraint." His welcome was genuine, his dedication to his guests complete.

Though in most ways Monticello represents hospitality at its best, it is an extreme example. Virginians pay attention to their homes but, unlike Jefferson, tend to spend judiciously

ABOVE: The 1850s farmhouse owned for sixty years by my maternal grandparents, the Keefers, sits happily amid acres of Virginia farmland.

rather than lavishly. They are by nature pragmatic. My mother is no exception. She collected quality pieces thoughtfully, over time. Disposable was not in her vocabulary. By her example, I learned the value not just of fine materials and workmanship but of timelessness.

When I was twelve my parents had bought their own land, and a few years later they embarked on building a house by Trueheart Poston, a Virginia architect with a deep knowledge of the state's colonial architecture, a deftness with both traditional and modern design, and a name as memorable as his disposition. For all their thrift and self-sufficiency, my parents knew when to hire a professional, an attribute I came to appreciate and emulate as I developed my own practice.

My mother's furnishing of our house was an exercise in building a collection intelligently and lovingly. She was allergic to sets of furniture, as am I. Trips to Mrs. Jackson's, an antique dealer's shop near downtown Lynchburg, were as regular a part of our family activities as church. You could say I grew up shaped by Jesus and antiques. I may be the family member in the design world but it's my younger brother, the pastor, who can beat me to the punch when identifying a good piece of furniture.

Mrs. Jackson's occupied an 1890s clapboard house that sat on a large shady corner lot and featured something rarely seen in Lynchburg: a koi pond. More memorable than the pond, though, or even the antiques, which were mostly English and American, some French, that the refined and gentle Mrs. Jackson sold, was the experience of being in the house itself. The house taught me a fundamental lesson about presence. Though I sensed immediately the effect its noble bearing had on me, it was over the course of many visits that I came to understand the roots of its power: high ceilings, fine moldings, beautiful proportions.

Gracious rooms begin with elegant architecture. I believe that the things that are attached to the walls—cabinetry, tilework, paneling—should be classic. And it's worth every penny to make sure they are well-executed, that the proportions are right, the joints are tight and smooth, the grout is even. When it comes to updating an interior, you don't want to have to tear out a shower or a wall of closets; the refreshing can come via furniture and fabrics.

It's not always a matter of money, it's about choices, and in the chapters that follow, I hope each project, by example, will guide you in making good ones. Within each chapter is a particular focus on a design principle that is a fundamental building block of my approach to shaping gracious rooms. I hope these principles will help you lay a strong foundation for an interior that inspires and endures.

For all the codified fundamentals of design and decoration, there are four guiding lights that, for me, make an interior turn the corner from house to home:

Make it interesting.

Make it beautiful.

Make it personal.

Make it welcoming and warm.

In life, a well-decorated room should feel like an invitation, something we all wish to offer and receive, a gesture that forms a relationship and is, I believe, the very definition of graciousness.

THE LIGHTNESS OF BEING

Whether we realize it or not, we each have a built-in light meter that, more than any particular style, steers the look and comfort level of our interiors. Some of us prefer dim and cozy. Others gravitate to dark and dramatic, and still others are drawn to bright and spare or light and elegant.

A house on a lake often adopts a darker, more woodsy aesthetic but there's no reason it has to. Not everyone heads to the lake for boating and fishing. Some simply want to be in an environment that's all about calm and quiet, where sunlight bouncing off the water floods rooms and lifts spirits.

This house reminds me of some Southern ladies I have known who are stylish and confident enough to pair a favorite old coat with a fashionable new dress. With its natural edge clapboard siding, the house reads as a rustic "cabin" on the outside, but its interior has the air of a refined cottage.

Even in a natural setting, there are ways to achieve elegance and put everyone at ease. Color is one. For the rooms that flow into each other—foyer, living room, dining room, kitchen—I chose a creamy white for the walls, capped by a warm beige for the ceilings. During the day, these rooms are bowls of sunshine; at night, they glow like a lantern. To me, white has a natural sophistication. Whether it's cool and modern or softly romantic, it elevates an interior. As does black.

The doors in this house are so handsome that I wanted to draw more attention to them, so they became smart black sentries. I love black as an accent color and try to weave it through an interior. Nothing pulls this off as well as ironwork, especially in a more informal setting by the lake or up in the mountains. Ironwork can be shaped into lyrical, natural lines or take on a more geometric form, like three-dimensional calligraphy. Here, I employed a combination in lamps, lanterns, chandeliers, curtain rods, a basket for firewood, table bases, spool chairs, a canopy bed, and the stair rail.

A palette doesn't just concern itself with color. Materials have everything to do with setting a tone. The television in the living room isn't housed in any old cupboard, but in an antique armoire from Brittany that has the most fabulous brass handles and studding. I love using hooked rugs in a country house; to me they are like putting fine American folk art underfoot. The artwork in the dining room is a charming old painted sign that's appropriate for a Georgia country house. It also happens to speak French.

Americans swoon over a European accent—and not just the kind you hear. I'm no exception. Introducing European antiques and materials into a room can make it more beguiling. The fabrics I first proposed for this house were almost too American, certainly too rustic. So instead of homespun for curtains, we stepped up to a Chelsea Textiles linen embroidered with sprigs of flowers for the living room, a lovely plaid from Holland & Sherry in the study, and another Chelsea Textiles fabric for the master bedroom.

The role of all the materials in this house, soft and otherwise, is the same: to convey a quiet sense of luxury. In each room, the color of the curtains is close to the wall color so the curtains don't make a bold statement. What pattern they have is also subtle. I've always thought the role of curtains should be to frame a view discreetly, not to distract from it.

PREVIOUS PAGE: Live edge siding stained slate gray bridges the rustic and the sophisticated.
RIGHT: An antique grandfather clock from Ainsworth-Noah stands sentry at the end of the entry, drawing the eye down the hall from the front door. A French buffet and bench upholstered in cotton provide places for both things and people to land. Balancing elegant imported pieces are antique American hooked rugs and fishing creels. A clipping from a tree outside gives the foyer a welcoming flourish of green.

PREVIOUS SPREAD:
Furnishings in deep natural
hues—wooden tables and an
armoire, leather chairs, a
wool hooked rug based on a
historic design—ground the
living room. Above table
level, handblown glass lamps,
an antique hobbyhorse,
glass apothecary bottles, a
wrought-iron floor lamp, and
a glass-sided lantern make
for an airier atmosphere.
RIGHT: An antique armoire
from France houses the
television, its handsome
bearing made more playful
by brass studs. A pair
of bobbin chairs that sit
before it are similarly
proud and lighthearted.

PREVIOUS SPREAD: In the dining room, French walnut armless chairs slipcovered in ecru linen with a blue monogram balance the rusticity of the antique trestle table. Curtains made of ticking and fixtures of wrought iron (curtain rods and lighting) are at once elegant and informal, as is the "Epicerie" sign. RIGHT: Antique English oak stools, the only natural wood in the kitchen, tuck under the island counter. In an otherwise all-white space, the beadboard backs of the upper cabinets are painted pale blue/gray to subtly set off their contents.

PREVIOUS SPREAD: In the
study, a coat of olive green
unifies woodwork, trim, a
bookshelf, and windows,
making the space simultaneously cozy and lofty. Curtains
in a windowpane wool, and a
wingchair and ottoman in
wool herringbone, extend the
subtle tone-on-tone palette,
ceding center stage to a bold
antique American hooked rug.
Botanical prints circle the
room at the same height,
lending eye-level interest to all
the walls. RIGHT: Beneath a
coffered ceiling that lends
intimacy, the master
bedroom is a sampler of
details that spark interest:
turned legs in different
profiles, a laced canopy, a
ratchet chair finished in
nailheads, a pair of counter-
poise swing-arm lamps.

THE INS AND OUTS OF SYMMETRY

Symmetry is a wonderful organizing tool. It brings order and balance to interiors. But, as with many design principles, it should be applied judiciously and creatively. Too much symmetry, as in a room where one half mirrors the other, can becalm a space. What you want is harmony, with interest.

◆ Even a space as straightforward as a bathroom benefits from a decorative flourish that complements its order. Here, I composed cabinetry, sinks, mirrors, and lighting in a symmetrical arrangement in keeping with the room's highly functional purpose. Decorative accessories on the counter and a fanciful Victorian stool add flair and a dose of asymmetry to the all-white space. A bathroom is the most intimate place in the house; it should never feel clinical.

◆ When a furniture arrangement is symmetrical, I always make sure the individual parts vary. In this house's living room, pairs of chairs flank a coffee table, but one pair is upholstered leather club chairs and the other is spool chairs with ticking-covered cushions. Framing the sofa are end tables and lamps. The lamps are the same; the tables are different (one round, one rectangular).

◆ Use furnishings architecturally to establish symmetry. For instance, a large armoire on one wall of this living room balances the wide opening to the dining room, extending the symmetry established by French doors flanking the fireplace.

◆ Two bedrooms in this house are mirror images of each other architecturally. Though the furniture arrangement is nearly identical in each, two different palettes of colors and materials give the rooms distinct personalities. With bedside tables and lamps, I like to mix and match: either the tables are the same but the lamps different, or the lamps are the same but the tables different. Scale is what makes them match.

OPPOSITE: In the cream-colored master bath, an antique hooked rug, Victorian stool, and branches in an apothecary jar add dashes of color and flashes of pattern and whimsy.

PREVIOUS SPREAD: In a guest bedroom, antique marble-topped bistro tables flank a four-poster bed; at its foot sits a grain bin that can hold extra bed linens. Hooked rugs relieve wall-to-wall sea-grass matting. ABOVE: Apart from their country charm, chicken wire–fronted vanity doors allow air to circulate around towels in the guest bathroom. OPPOSITE: In another bedroom, linen cushions soften a caned settee, and a flea market plant stand lifts greenery to the daylight. FOLLOWING SPREAD: Natural wicker sofas and painted Kennedy rockers are gathered around a limestone-topped iron table on the screened porch. The bronze drinks tables have twig bases.

A HOUSE OF SUBSTANCE

Every house has a message to deliver, even before you get started with the decorating. Some houses will give you a definite sense of direction. Others will offer no guidance at all, which can be liberating or disabling, depending on how much you're a fan of a clean slate. Encountering a house for the first time is just like making a new acquaintance—if you want the relationship to blossom, the important thing is to look and listen, to be open and curious.

Decorating a house is a coming together of an environment that is (more than likely) new to you and the preferences you've been refining, consciously or not, all your life. Every project involves more decisions than you can ever imagine. I've always felt that the more thought that goes into making those decisions, the longer you live contentedly with them.

So invest some time in studying your house, its structure and materials, its setting and orientation in the landscape, the way light and sound move through it. And then remind yourself of what makes you happiest in spaces, whether it's saturated color, a comfy chair, or a tub with a view. Every mistake I've ever encountered, or made myself, came from rushing. Take your time so you can be true to the house and yourself.

This house was built in the early part of the twentieth century, when materials were substantial and the standard of architectural detailing was high. Its stone exterior and vaguely Tudor/Norman style exert a certain masculine sobriety. I'm all for handsome and, in fact, gravitate to darker wood and subdued colors, especially grays and browns. No insult to Mom, but I always have to remind her, "Gray *is* a color."

If pressed to capture my approach to design in a single phrase, it would be "Make it beautiful." More important than any style is the feeling you get from an interior. There's nothing better than having guests walk into your house and say, without yet being able to identify why, "I just love it here."

As remarkable as the antiques in the entrance hall of this house are, especially the round marquetry table and the Italian baroque mirror, it's the taxidermy swan that melts my heart; it tips the mood of the foyer from formal to fun. It's like dressing the dinner table in its finest, only to serve burgers and beans. Placing a ketchup bottle amid the cut crystal and polished silver is a little whimsical, and you can bet it immediately puts everyone at ease.

For all the dark oak trim, wrought iron, and deeply stained floors that lend this house seriousness, there is something in every room that gives it a joyous lift. In the living room, it's the wonderful color persimmon, subtler than red, more sophisticated than orange, that turns up in the fabrics that my associate, Elizabeth, and I selected (the same hue enriches the inside of one of my favorite pieces of furniture ever—an extraordinary Swedish secretary from the turn of the eighteenth century). In the breakfast area, it's a curved banquette with scalloped trim. In the back hall, it's a floor of hexagonal tiles from Paris Ceramics whose random coloration makes a lively welcome mat.

In any profession, the more you know what you're doing, the more you want to try something different. It's not actually risky behavior; it's natural growth. Taking chances in decorating means making intuitive choices informed by deep experience. That's how thick Lucite tables ended up alongside a neoclassical Italian bergère in the living room. And how a myriad of materials and textures—bronze and shagreen, linen and cashmere, onyx and nickel—came together in the sun-room and adjacent bar.

My biggest "risk" was in the dining room. Dining rooms are, in my mind, perfect candidates for special treatment due to their less frequent, primarily nighttime use. They can handle standing apart from other living spaces. Much as I wanted to create an atmospheric setting, I was after something more unexpected than de Gournay or Zuber wallpaper, exquisite though they are.

I turned to artist Michael Dines to create a mural that encircled the room. I love the quiet mood, the soft palette, and the connection to nature that characterize his work. No wonder his paintings regularly turn up in my interiors. This was the first mural he had ever done, and he accomplished what I had been dreaming of. Being in that room is like gliding through open fields at dawn or dusk—totally transporting.

PAGE 35: In the entry foyer, nature in the form of loose blooming greenery and a tall white swan tempers the serious and elegant aspect of an antique commode from Lombardy and a heavily carved and partially gilded Italian baroque mirror. PREVIOUS PAGES: The delicate patterning of a handwoven Karabagh rug from the turn of the last century provides a contrast to strong forms in iron and wood, a tonal link to the wall tapestry and a sophisticated welcome mat in the entry. Picking up on the segmented curve of the stairs is a rare Italian neoclassical pedestal table with an octagonal base and dodecagonal marquetry top. OPPOSITE: A Gustavian rococo secretary with a particularly exuberant interior is the engaging and tall Swedish model attracting attention in the living room.

PREVIOUS SPREAD: The living room is a balance of highs, lows, and in-betweens: a tall secretary and columnar lamps, tables of varying heights, and stools readily available for extra seating. OPPOSITE: Lustrous antique leather and wood surfaces, complete with curves and curls, stand in contrast to the light-absorbing cotton velvet upholstery of the sofa behind. ABOVE: Acrylic drinks tables drop a fresh contemporary note into a suite of furniture that includes a giltwood bergère, an antique fruitwood table, and a pair of consoles composed of iron railings topped with limestone.

ABOVE: Silk curtains extend the shimmer of a Venetian mirror above a circa 1720 Dutch rosewood marquetry cabinet in the dining room. OPPOSITE: The moss green silk velvet of the custom dining chairs around a Rose Tarlow table picks up the soft hues in artist Michael Dine's interpretation of the indigenous landscape. FOLLOWING SPREAD: Leaves in various forms connect the sunroom to the garden: in wrought iron on the standing lamps, in gilt tole on the pendant fixture, in embroidery on the leading edge of the linen curtains, in crewelwork on the pillows, and in living color via a ficus tree.

PREVIOUS SPREAD: A cove crown molding with a bead that creates a delicate shadow line integrates the single wall-hung cabinet. The stove hood is plaster with a Calacatta-marble edge to match the counters and backsplash. ABOVE: Raised panel and leaded glass cabinet doors distinguish the china pantry from the rest of the kitchen cabinetry. OPPOSITE: Bracketed marble shelves display a collection of Victorian jasperware. FOLLOWING SPREAD: Scallops add a lighthearted detail to a curved banquette in the breakfast room (LEFT) while variegated tiles from Paris Ceramics contribute a lively texture to the rear foyer (RIGHT).

LIVING WITH COLLECTIONS

Collections are such wonderful, tangible expressions of people's passions. They add tremendous personality to an interior. Like many things that are idiosyncratic, though, they need to be properly presented to shine.

◆ Start by turning a critical eye on the things you have. Simply owning numerous examples of one thing does not necessarily constitute a collection. You may have ended up with dozens of owl figurines from having once casually mentioned that you liked the wise bird, but that does not mean you are obliged to scatter them throughout the house like blinking spy cameras. If sentimentality gets in the way of an honest edit, enlist a friend to help.

◆ Spreading one motif everywhere dilutes its effect. One client of mine was so enamored of flowers that she failed to realize nearly everything she owned had some floral aspect. Via some heavy pruning and select replanting, her blossoms flourished.

◆ Concentrating a collection is one of the most effective ways to show it off. In this house, we custom-made a glass-topped coffee table with a leather pullout tray for displaying groupings of engraved silver compacts, cameos, and boxes in mother-of-pearl and tortoiseshell. In the kitchen, marble shelves highlight a collection of Victorian jasperware.

◆ Sometimes a collection simply needs to be recast. Framing plaster medallions in shadow boxes lined with champagne-colored silk gave them much more presence. Grouping them in the powder room allowed them to lend even more impact and made them accessible for closer study.

◆ If you're just getting started collecting, train your eye to be discriminating. My mother loves porcelain and can identify every mark. I can't always cite the exact provenance of an object, but having been dragged through many an antique shop by her, I learned how to tell at a glance whether something was good. Look, look, and look some more. And then look with a different eye when it comes time to display your prized objects.

OPPOSITE: Furnishing the powder room with an antique sewing table lent further weight and context to the collection of plaster medallions that line the walls.

LEFT: An Etro ad featuring a layered pattern was the inspiration for the walnut-paneled library. A sofa upholstered in bronze silk velvet and club chairs in camel-colored wool balance the paisley-patterned Persian Tabriz carpet and de Le Cuona curtains. At the center of it all, a custom-made ebonized cherry coffee table displays a collection of antique boxes in a leather-lined drawer.

OPPOSITE: A pair of gilt-framed wing chairs provide a spot for reading by the window in the master bedroom. The painting is by Michael Dines. Curtains in Holland & Sherry wool are appliquéd in a motif far bolder than the overall pattern of the Tabriz carpet. ABOVE: Cameos framed in groups form a rhythm above the bedframe upholstered in ivory wool. In a restful palette of smoky hues and mixed woods, the pale crisp color of the bed and bench are fresh and inviting.

ABOVE: Paneling painted a warm taupe unites a master bathroom composed of two adjoining spaces. Even the tub gets the same treatment. The patterned mosaic floor introduces a contrast in scale while marble baseboards are both pretty and practical. OPPOSITE: The Venetian chandelier is vintage and the taps are traditional but the Jonathan Browning sconces and a frameless glass shower door are contemporary. FOLLOWING SPREAD: A palette of cream accented with blue unites the daughter's suite where custom cupboards form a niche for the sink (LEFT) and a shapely headboard is embellished with custom embroidery (RIGHT).

ABOVE: Antique English oak, leaded glass, brushed black granite, and plenty of pewter
evoke a stylish tavern in the pantry/bar adjacent to the lower-level club room.
OPPOSITE: Mattaliano's Jean-Michel Frank sectional, upholstered in textured Donegal
chenille and served by bronze and parchment tables, sets a handsome, comfortable
tone for the paneled club room. Wild mustang photographs are by Kimberly Curyl.

FOR THE GENERATIONS

Everyone loves a house by a lake. Being by the water brings a playfulness to everyday life. Total refreshment is just a skip and a dive away. For others, simply looking out at the water is enough to make one's cares disappear. Just as yawning breeds yawning, it's easy to catch the calm of tranquil waters.

A house by the water delivers happiness for all ages, making it an ideal getaway, where family can gather on vacation, for holidays, or for weekends. It is refuge and fun camp in one, for multiple generations to use now and for future generations to hold dear. Above all, it is a treasure chest of happy times that become family lore.

When a lake house is not just a summer camp, but a year-round second home, its interiors need to be relaxed, yet still substantial. No tacked-up curtains and flimsy cots. You want the sofas and armchairs to encourage stretching out and curling up, so they need generous proportions and hard-wearing yet pretty fabrics like chenille that are soft to the touch. A coffee table can invite not just board games and bowls of snacks—not to mention perched feet—and still be handsome. Other tables need to be able to handle cool glasses and warm mugs without worry. Let user-friendly materials, durable finishes, and inviting shapes be your guide. It's all about ease, but never about sloppiness.

And it's also about a warm, distinctly American feel. I wanted the pores of this house to be infused with hospitality. Hooked and other hand-knotted rugs, the smaller ones antique, the larger ones custom-made, offer the perfect padding for bare and socked feet. In keeping with the informality of a lake house, nearly every chandelier and floor lamp is wrought of iron, as are the curtain rods, and table lamps are fashioned of rustic crocks, wood balusters, and glass blown in large simple shapes.

The key to a well-furnished second home is to provide all of the elements of a more formal house dressed down in more relaxed materials, patterns, and forms. I love the playfulness, history, and silhouette of a bobbin chair almost as much as I love the friendliness of a check-patterned fabric. The combination, which I put together for side chairs in the living room, is as delicious, and as American, as apple pie. In a similar vein, I turned to a subtle linen plaid for roman shades in the kitchen and a small-scale plaid, layered over a tiny checked bed skirt, for pillow and duvet covers in the master bedroom. When it comes to pattern, I always opt for calm over drama. I prefer to allow the eye to roam over a room rather than to stop it in its tracks.

Ironically, at a time when anyone can obtain anything online, interiors can easily end up looking generic rather than individualized. I never want a room to feel like it could have been ordered soup-to-nuts from one source and drop-shipped into place. Every space should have a one-of-a-kind object or treatment that makes it distinct.

What brings character to the kitchen in this house, in addition to the custom cabinetry and exposed wood beams, are three antique glass French cloches suspended over the island. Not only do they have a graceful shape and dramatic scale, but they are timeless—the kind of fixture I would have loved fifteen years ago and will still love fifteen years from now.

PAGE 68: On the porch, comfortable iron furniture forms a conversation group, while traditional wooden rockers offer a view of the lake. OPPOSITE: High in the double-height living room, a twin-ringed chandelier picks up on the second-story ocular windows. Beyond the bobbin chairs upholstered in a checked linen, a custom armoire with an antiqued finish holds the television.

TAMING A LARGE ROOM

The great room has dominated the American house for the past twenty-five years. Some are the comfortable centers of entertaining and family living they were intended to be; others are, well, not so great. A room needs more than size to be a space that inspires pride and attracts family members to spend time in it.

◆ It's important to anchor double-height rooms and other large-volume spaces with substantial furniture. Here I upholstered a pair of club chairs and a large sofa, eighty-nine inches long, with skirts that go to the floor to ground them visually in the space. The weightiness of the sofa is balanced by the animated linear form of a pair of bobbin chairs and the open frames of the iron coffee table base and antique wooden side tables.

◆ To prevent this pale living room with lightly-textured plaster coat walls from floating upward, I ringed the walls with wainscoting painted a weightier dark gray. Aside from its power to alter scale, wood wainscoting is a very practical wall treatment, especially in vacation houses.

◆ A patterned rug, here a hand-knotted flatweave in an informal, almost quiltlike motif, both establishes the plane of the floor and balances the solid forms of the upholstered furniture. Together the rug and furniture ground the room.

◆ High, vaulted spaces need to be filled as well as anchored. Here a custom chandelier of concentric iron rings occupies the airy top half of the living room.

◆ A fireplace with significant architectural presence will overwhelm any small piece of furniture placed next to it. In this case, I designed an armoire that has enough presence to balance the door on the opposite side of the hearth and serves the practical purpose of housing a television.

OPPOSITE: The medium scale of a diamond-patterned flat-weave rug pulls together the tiny houndstooth and small checks of the chair upholstery as well as the large parquet pattern of the wood-topped coffee table. Linen curtains hand-printed with ferns frame the view to the outdoors.

PREVIOUS SPREAD: Barley twist bar stools upholstered in a floral-printed linen pull up to a massive soapstone-topped island in the open kitchen. The three bell-cloche lanterns are French antiques. Long narrow tiles for the backsplash depart from standard subway tile dimensions. ABOVE: The soft luster of the pewter collection suits the worn paint finish of a country cabinet in the breakfast room. OPPOSITE: Seat pads in brown linen with green welts and ties lend more comfort to Windsor chairs set around the chunky oak breakfast table.

ABOVE, LEFT: The plaid pattern of antique sieves reappears in the breakfast room's linen curtains and the kitchen's roman shades. ABOVE, RIGHT: Baskets, bowls, and pewter, here on and under an antique oak cabriole-leg table, are both decorative and practical. OPPOSITE: On the porch a celebration of patina in three materials: metal, wood, and terra-cotta.

ABOVE: Detailed cabinetry, hex tiles of flamed limestone, framed botanicals, and a cushioned bench elevate a utilitarian back entry hall that houses coat and broom closets. OPPOSITE: The barn red cabinetry and honed black granite counters of the utility room suit the activities of laundry, potting herbs, and floral arranging equally well.

PREVIOUS SPREAD: In the master bedroom, yellow wing chairs set off by deep taupe wainscoting are positioned by the window (LEFT) to catch light falling over a shoulder, while a king-size oak canopy bed (RIGHT) anchors the center of the room. The varying patterns of floral curtains, tattersall bed linens, and a custom hand-hooked rug unite in a warm palette of yellows, tans, and browns. ABOVE: Ochre pigment was added to the plaster in the master bath to produce a golden hue. OPPOSITE: A wood base for the tub grounds it to the honed stone floor.

OPPOSITE: In a guest bedroom, delicate antlers set off a stylized antelope head above a French Academie iron bed. Walnut and wicker tables flanking the bed support matching lamps fashioned from balusters and topped by linen shades. ABOVE: An old crock becomes a lamp and a pitcher a vase for blooming branches atop an antique trestle table, which is set next to a bed with a headboard upholstered in a Rogers & Goffigon striped linen. At the foot of the bed sits an antique trunk with wonderful strap hinges and folkloric painting.

ABOVE: An installation of quirky birds on individual perches by artist Chris
Condon, all hand-carved, turns a hall leading to a mudroom into a destination.
OPPOSITE: Iron swivel bar stools upholstered in paprika windowpane wool pull up
to a bar tucked under an arch of a stair hall opening to the lower-level TV room.

GRAND WITH GRACE

Nothing is as glorious as big, beautiful rooms, provided they are truly beautiful and not just big. And when making a room an inviting space, nothing matters so much as good proportions. Not everyone will consciously notice the details of scale that come into play, but everyone will feel their effects. There is a sense of tranquility and grace in a well-proportioned space.

I am always grateful when the blank canvas I am given comes with well-scaled rooms. Not every house has them, but there are ways of refining any space to lend it more poise. Before any decorating can begin, it's important to get the architectural details right. Once the furnishings are installed and you're sitting on a sofa surveying the room, you want the door surrounds and fireplace and paneling to feel like strong supporters of all the softer elements. Beauty begins with good bone structure.

Big houses in general present big challenges, because people simply feel more at ease in spaces that are more intimate. It's not just a matter of filling rooms up. The rooms need to invite you in, make you comfortable, and provide what you need. Just like a good host.

This is quite a large house, 12,000 square feet, which is not unusual for the kind of residence in Atlanta that was put up by builders in the late 1980s and early 1990s. Unfortunately, that period of construction tended to be long on supersizing and short on charm. I find big Sheetrock rooms with basic trim "undercooked" and unappealing. It was my good fortune to collaborate with the architects Pak Heydt and Associates, who agreed that the house needed a big injection of architectural gravitas.

Using paint and color to highlight boldly scaled doorframes and disguise less successful architectural details helps any house mature into a more sophisticated presence. In the entry hall, the architects installed beams and I framed a new front door with geometric leaded glass windows made

PREVIOUS PAGE: The sculptural quality of an antique silver-leafed grotto chair can be seen from all angles in the stair hall. RIGHT: Silk curtains on a brass rod spanning the front door soften the architecture of the entry foyer. The straight lines of an eighteenth-century lacquered mirror and a Louis XVI walnut cabinet contrast with the scalloped frame and cabriole legs of an antique Venetian settee that sits opposite. Bridging them in color is a Persian Malayer rug.

by the late Pat Vloebergh, a local artisan who had a rare gift for her craft. If there was leaded glass restoration work to be done in the historical houses of Atlanta, she was the one everyone turned to.

I introduce leaded glass in many of my projects (sometimes in windows, often in cabinetry) because it lends refinement and an Old World quality not found in standard wood-frame muntins. For the same reason, I chose to pave the floor of the entry with reclaimed European limestone. The variation in the color of the pavers is subtle and beautiful. Unlike a polished marble floor, the effect is softer and more informal, dressy without being overdone. Most of all, it's welcoming. I was always taught that good manners begin with a gracious introduction. I think that applies every bit as much to houses as to people.

Decorating large rooms presents particular challenges. I understand the impulse to select big-scaled furniture, but that's like dressing a banquet table with only oversize chargers. The effect is flat and lifeless. Every room, no matter its size, needs furnishings in a variety of scale and materials to spark a visual conversation.

Even a formally arranged room can be given a friendlier character. Absent guests who bring it to life, a dining room can be the loneliest place in the house, especially if it adopts a stiff bearing. I knew a treasured antique dining table would be the centerpiece of this room, so I had a matelassé tablecloth made for it, and that softened the space both literally and atmospherically. In the same vein, I replaced a traditional white mantelpiece with something warmer—a carved wooden one, waxed to a soft luster.

Rooms that are grand above all else may suit the White House, but they're not in tune with the life most of us live these days. Though this living room is cavernous, not only long and wide but tall, it feels more inviting than imposing because it offers up a choice of distinct areas in which to settle.

Again, architectural elements—columns, paneling, niches, deep and grand doorframes, and a wide plain frieze above the crown molding—bring a more human scale to the room. Beyond that, it's the furniture plan that sets up intimate conversation areas. Especially in a space this large, I like to pull the furniture away from the periphery and activate the center. Two generous sofas are the anchors around which smaller tables and chairs can orbit. After all, who doesn't prefer a lively dance to a room lined with wallflowers?

OPPOSITE: The half-round shape of the custom banquette upholstered in silk mohair suits its position in a room, the stair hall, which is full of movement. Its graceful curves, along with the cupped shell backs of the grotto chairs, stand in contrast to the straight lines of the ribbed walls. A Plexiglas pedestal for the Empire bronze clock allows it to float at the same height as an Italian painting in a gilded frame. A Turkish Sivas carpet pulls all the tones together.

LEFT: A pair of sofas form the boundary of a more intimate space in the living room within which smaller pieces like a bergère in ivory silk and an antique burled walnut table can easily shift. Console tables behind each sofa provide a home to smaller objects and put lamps and books within reach. An extra tall wrought-iron floor lamp extends upward into the lofty blue space like a skyscraper poking above the horizon line.

RIGHT: The shape of barrel-backed chairs in ivory quilted silk echoes the base of the lyre table. Maggie Hasbrouk's painting of a calla lily, its black background serving as a dark window within a niche, hangs above an antique Italian chest of drawers. Just as paneling breaks up the expanse of the living room walls, a Greek key tape modulates the solid form of the sofas.

THE TRANSFORMERS:
COLOR AND PAINT

Paint has always been a designer's not-so-secret weapon. For me, it's an ever-reliable tool for highlighting good features in an interior and disguising the unfortunate ones. Hand in hand with the right color, there simply is no easier, or more affordable, way to change a space or create a mood.

◆ When I confront a detail I'm not crazy about, I always consider painting it before I turn to tearing it out. The chair rail in the front hall of this house was ill-proportioned. To minimize its presence, I painted it the same warm pewter gray as the matte walls. By receding into the overall background color, the chair rail allows the eye to focus on the furniture placed before it.

◆ For a room that connects multiple spaces, such as the stair hall in this house, I usually select a light color and paint the walls the same shade as the trim to create a sense of flow. If there is already a lot of activity in a space, you want the color to act as a calming agent. A good neutral, like the pale gray I chose here, will also work well with almost any color connecting to it.

◆ I view a dining room as an opportunity to immerse a space (walls, doors, windows, trim) in one rich, deep color. Since a dining room is used mostly at night and, one hopes, in candlelight, why not have it project a bit of romance and mystery? To balance the deep gray-brown of this house's dining room, other furnishings, such as the chairs, carpet, roman shades, and artwork, swung to the lighter side of the spectrum.

◆ Color alone can rescale a room and redirect the eye. In the living room of this house, I painted all the paneling a pale blue, leaving the vaulted ceiling white. Through simple placement of color, the room gains a more intimate scale at floor level, yet the airy volume above is allowed to soar. Glossy black doors introduce a tall, dark, and handsome element to the room, helping to ground the huge volume of space.

OPPOSITE: Nature thrives in a bay of the living room framed by columns. Behind a tapestry-upholstered chair and a gilded faux bois table supporting an orchid, an antique garden urn planted with ivy and palm fills a niche.

PREVIOUS SPREAD: A matelassé tablecloth lends a grand mahogany dining table more informal dress for every day. An existing set of twelve dining chairs was refinished and reupholstered in a silvery blue fabric with big blossoms centered in the frame of the chair backs. Lynn Geesaman's photographs of gardens float above the mantelpiece. LEFT: In the breakfast room, cream linen slipcovers temper the weight of barley twist-frame chairs and a table with an unusual columned base and carved stretcher. Wrought-iron lighting and curtain hardware add a calligraphic accent to the white space.

RIGHT: Oversize subway tile suits the scale of a kitchen that easily accommodates a Le Cornue range and hood and cabinets that reach to the high ceiling. Vintage Holophane pendants with polished aluminum cladding light the generous island, whose rounded open ends make a collection of ironstone readily accessible. Additional pendant fixtures of polished nickel and milk glass maintain the feel of a kitchen in a grand old house.

RIGHT: A sofa in olive chenille, a pair of vintage Italian wing chairs in a stylized floral, simple wood tables and stools, plain linen curtains, and a gray wool sisal carpet maintain a casual air in the family room. The photographic painting of a forest scene is by John Folsom.

ABOVE: Bedside tables, one with a worn silver-leaf finish, the other a petite English chest of drawers, hit just the right reaching distance from bed. The wings of the headboard define a niche for the bed as well as provide a headrest for reading. Clear Murano glass lamps and crystal chandelier drops sow additional glints of light. OPPOSITE: Silk curtains in a broad stripe provide a bold yet pretty backdrop for a French chair and ottoman and an antique armoire.

DRESSING UP, DRESSING DOWN

We live in an informal age. People show up to the theater in loungewear, share their dinner tables with electronic devices, and communicate via acronym. I would no more go to a client meeting in a slouchy outfit than I would deprive my house of fresh flowers. Call me old-fashioned or Southern or both, but I believe dressing nicely and furnishing one's house thoughtfully show respect for others, not to mention for oneself.

That's not to say that presentation—of person or home—need be formal. I'm less for standing on ceremony than for celebrating the lovely things in life, like antiques and art, flowers and books, sunlight and candlelight. I want to make rooms people want to be in, interiors that make you sit up to take notice of interesting things and sit back to luxuriate in comfort.

An easy elegance is always my goal. To that end, I take formal principles and dress them informally, or at least in a blend of traditional and more contemporary forms and materials. In the living room of this house, symmetry guides the furniture plan. A pair of identical sofas frames the fireplace, matching console tables occupy the niches flanking it, and twin antique chairs cozy up to the hearth.

Despite the formal furniture arrangement, a relaxed quality prevails because the individual elements are anything but stiff. The Oriental rug is an Oushak, but its colors are so muted as to register as a warm monotone, a soft extension of the wide-plank floors. The leather chairs and all of the wood tables are rustic, and the arrangements on and above the console tables are distinct compositions of objects, lamps, and art.

PAGE 113: A blue shutter and an antique tapestry, equally rich in tone if opposite in texture, frame a French ratchet chair, upholstered in white linen to accentuate its contours and charming "ears." PREVIOUS SPREAD: Cool greens and blues are seeded throughout the living room, which is otherwise a composition in white warmed by natural wood and an antique Oushak carpet. ABOVE, LEFT: The straight architectural lines of a French gessoed mirror are as clean as the curvaceous antique dresser above which it hangs. ABOVE, RIGHT: Drawings, lamps, and objects form a collage of gold above an antiqued walnut console from Formations, one of two that flank the fireplace. OPPOSITE: A deep sofa with down pillows and a thick throw is the definition of cozy comfort. The table is an English antique from Linda Horsley.

ABOVE: A collection of gold-framed sketches, floated on silk matting the same chocolate color as the dining room walls, animates the space above an Italian Directoire fruitwood credenza.
OPPOSITE: Two sets of fig-colored chairs, one upholstered in linen velvet, the other in washed linen with an embroidered medallion, circle a table draped in ivory matelassé. The slender profiles of a Louis XVI mirror and an iron and wood chandelier are equally elegant.

The sofas are the very definition of grace and comfort: overscaled and upholstered in soft white linen slipcovers with waterfall skirts, a la Belgian designer and unrivaled tastemaker Axel Vervoordt. Who can resist a sofa you can stretch out on, with plenty of pillows and a plush throw to snuggle up in.

Vervoordt's interiors are often on a grand scale and feature extraordinary objects, but for all of their sophistication, they still deliver what everyone hungers for at home: harmonious rooms that feed the mind and calm the soul. His spaces offer a tip: sometimes all it takes to tilt the scale in that direction is the addition of a single organic thing.

Obvious as it may seem, nothing makes a room come to life like something living. It's amazing how much a simple urn of spring branches just beginning to blossom or a vase of wildflowers can lift an interior. And those are at most people's fingertips, just outside in the yard or along the roadside. More exotic choices may come from a florist, but even the supermarket can be a steady supplier.

In this house, nature sets up camp in nearly every room: a mound of moss on the coffee table, a potted fiddle leaf fig tree in a corner of the living room, a big bowl of limes on the dining room table, potted herbs in the kitchen, cut flowers in the powder room, small leafy plants in the master bedroom. Not only are they all a balm, as if they were injecting the air with extra oxygen, but they are welcome splashes of green in a neutral palette of mostly cream, tan, and taupe.

All colors are in nature but, in my experience, greens and blues are the colors people are most drawn to. Everyone who enters this living room admires the verdigris of the vessels on the sofa table, the teal of the chandelier, the many shades from emerald to ocean in the tapestry pillows and footstool. But they are absolutely crazy for the turquoise shutters.

Sometimes you just have to take the risk and make a bold move. The three formal French doors topped by fanlights were always pretty and highly functional. Light pours through them, and they provide access to an enclosed patio. But adding new rustic shutters faux-finished in heavenly blue was like adding a cape to a superhero. The room broke out of a traditional mold and soared.

OPPOSITE: A high-back library chair cozies up to the family room fireplace opposite an English roll-arm sofa upholstered in oyster gray wool. FOLLOWING SPREAD: An adjustable antique floor lamp serves a pair of wing chairs in charcoal wool, which flank a round tavern table. A rug of braided rush extends the floor color in a softer layer.

PARTNERS IN DESIGN:
FORMAL AND INFORMAL

Just as an interior gains depth when it embraces a combination of antique and modern furnishings, so too does it benefit from dovetailing of the formal and informal. The degree to which it swings in either direction is a matter of both personal taste and behavior.

◆ When I love the form of a piece of furniture, particularly a chair, I look to strengthen that form by using a solid fabric for upholstery. For instance, a patterned textile might have swallowed the odd but charming earlike wings of the ratchet chair in this living room. A simple white linen allows its contours to shine.

◆ Rooms populated by many legs (like a dining room filled with chairs) benefit from a simple form in their midst. In this living room, the clean modern lines of two generous sofas offset the range of wooden antiques. Each sofa's seat is tight, not separate as a cushion, and its white linen slipcover, skirted to the floor, features just the right degree of relaxed fit.

◆ A round table warms up even the most formal dining room. With no head of table, guest and host are on equal footing, sending a convivial signal that puts everyone at ease. Plus a round table encourages conversation in all directions. For entertaining, two round tables (if your dining room is a typical size, one permanent table and a portable one that can be stored) rather than one long one make for a lively, friendly gathering.

◆ It's lovely to have special table linens for special occasions, but a dining table benefits from a tablecloth it can wear every day. Draping it in an informal fabric like a heavy matelassé lends it gravitational pull that a bare table in a dining room rarely exerts.

◆ I love mixing chairs at a dining table, like the two sets of antique chairs here. Though their shapes are different, their uniform golden wood frames and taupe linen upholstery unite them as a team. The chairs look custom-embroidered, but the stitched detail is simply a section of a Travers fabric that was centered in the framework of the chair back.

OPPOSITE: The marble basin in the powder room stands out like a shell on a volcanic beach. Wrought-iron sconces, wall-mounted taps, and the hand-forged base supporting the stone counter give chic a rustic edge.

PREVIOUS SPREAD: A farmhouse sink and adjacent dishwasher take up the sunniest position in the kitchen, the bay window. An island table made of reclaimed wood, linen-slipcovered counter stools, and wrought-iron shelf supports, sconces, chandelier, and knobs all project a casual air. ABOVE: Mismatched dish cupboards, their interiors painted a deep olive green, are the perfect relay station between kitchen and dining room. OPPOSITE: Shelving and tile form a three-dimensional backsplash that incorporates the stove hood.

ABOVE: Lighting for the sink area is kept clean and simple: unobscured daylight augmented by shaded sconces. The deep counter in the bay window leaves space for potted herbs to thrive. OPPOSITE: Antique doors fronting shallow pantry cupboards line the passageway between the dining room and kitchen.

OPPOSITE: A hand-forged wrought-iron canopy bed with upholstered headboard lifts the bed toward the reclaimed oak–lined tray ceiling of the master bedroom. A pair of linen-slipcovered chairs are low and wide, as is the iron bench with tufted cushion. ABOVE: French oak wood shelves built into either side of the fireplace visually connect to the mantelpiece and the ceiling. Tucking the TV into the shelving allows the fireplace to take center stage.

ODE TO A VIEW

For all of its leafiness and beautiful old neighborhoods, Atlanta can get so steamy as to reduce even the sturdiest residents to a wilted state. That is, if the traffic doesn't engulf them first. No wonder many folks choose to escape to the hills, specifically to lakeside retreats in the rolling terrain where Georgia borders South and North Carolina. This natural setting is a peaceful world away, and a house there should match its environment.

When a house benefits from a beautiful view, I want its interior to support a seamless bond between inside and out—this is especially true for a beautiful view of water, which creates its own magical light and space. Because this house is built on a hillside, every room takes advantage of lake vistas. The moment you step in the front door, you look across, down, and out to water. Yet it is not a house of glass. Though recently built, it uses natural materials both old and new to knit itself into its setting.

Having drawn comfort time and again from the hills and fields around my own family's farm in Virginia, I have always believed that the closer we stay to nature, the more at home, in every sense, we feel. During long walks on the farm, I absorbed right through my feet the muted greens and grays to which I gravitate today. Green is often thought of as a cool color, but in fact there's nothing quite so warm and soothing as a soft green. Who wouldn't want to capture in a room the deliciously restorative feeling of lying in the grass under the canopy of a tree on a summer afternoon?

A muted light green seemed like just the right color to complement the barnlike qualities of this house. Using that same green uniformly, on everything from the board-and-batten walls of the entry balcony to built-in cupboards to every inch of kitchen cabinetry to beadboard throughout the house, balanced the rougher texture and deeper tones of the rustic wood timbers. You are always aware of the framework of this house. It's as if the trees outside decided to straighten up and offer their services as key supporting players inside. The wood is a direct link to nature, as well as to the past.

Wood in various forms—raw, stained, painted—is a distinctly American material. Much as I admire the elegance of plaster and stone European houses, I believe wood makes a house feel like a home. From log cabins to converted barns, from country cottages to Victorian mansions, wood is a timeless material that allows houses to be enormously expressive. For interiors, I love the rhythm, pattern, practicality, and friendliness of painted boards. Nearly every room in this house other than the living room is lined with painted wood. Beadboard, whether narrow or wide, and wainscoting lend instant depth and character to a space. They capture an easygoing yet enduring quality as iconically American as the split-rail fences that first appeared in this country in colonial Virginia.

I wanted American country to slip into this house with the casual ease of a vase of wildflowers. For a built-in cupboard, I chose iron strap hinges and knobs for their straightforward graphic quality. The talented Charles Calhoun, Atlanta's noteworthy metalworker, made the hinged fireplace screen, chandeliers, and other light fixtures all of iron. Antique quilts and feed sacks became new cushion covers. Above a hickory bed made locally, I hung a vintage sign that I found at a flea market; in jaunty white letters marked with reflective dots it spells out WHISTLE. It makes everyone smile.

Throughout the house, fern fronds, Queen Anne's lace, branches, and wisps of vines remind you that you are just one step away from the outdoors. Inside with the windows open or out on the screened porch, you hear not only the birds, but the echo of voices skipping across the water— a single tweet or shriek perfectly conveys the joy of unfettered lake living. Good decorating never considers just the visual; it addresses all the senses.

PAGE 135: The upper deck of the boathouse is a favorite lakeside perch. Sturdy teak furniture (a pair of chaise longues and a dining table and chairs) lets the view steal the show. RIGHT: In the living room, age and nature in all their imperfection are perfect decorating partners. Pillows made from an old quilt pick up the cool tones of the Appalachian Landscape painting by Michael Dines, while a hand-carved burl wood bowl strikes the same amber hue as the leather chairs. Above a tin-lined cubby for firewood, eighteenth-century firkins populate the shelves.

OPPOSITE: The cheery barn red entry door opens to a balcony overlooking the living room. An antique runner from Budapest offers a note of rustic elegance. Board-and-batten walls and beadboard ceilings are more tailored than the rustic wood framework of the house but just as friendly. ABOVE: Benches are ideal hallway furniture, narrow enough to not obstruct passage but great organizers of all sorts of things that come and go, like totes and boots. Above this one hangs a collection of French vintage animal prints used as teaching tools.

TAKE YOUR CUE
FROM THE SETTING

An interior should never compete with a spectacular view. Instead, it should embrace it through color, materials, and furniture arrangement.

◆ When a house's public rooms orient to a beautiful view, take a lighter hand with window treatments, or even dispense with them altogether. In this living room, I installed one continuous iron rod just beneath a horizontal beam and designed an unlined linen curtain that's like a scrim; it extends the length of the room, breaking the glare but never fully blocking the light or the view.

◆ All colors can be found in nature, but those we associate with earthy tones—greens, grays, browns—subtly knit an interior into a natural setting. Your interior needn't turn glum and muddy, though; it's all about choosing colors that have an interesting dimension and are neither too dark nor too bright. Reserve the hues at the more extreme ends of the spectrum for accents.

◆ It's a natural impulse to place a bed opposite a window with a spectacular view. But too often that means bright light will beam directly onto the bed pillows and the heads occupying them! Better to position a bed at a right angle to the window so it benefits from light falling across it and still offers a chance to enjoy the view.

◆ Turn to botanicals to bring the outside in. Even in a non-floral season like late fall, you can find vines and branches in your own yard or alongside the road to trim and place in antique crocks, pitchers, and bottles. Pressed flowers and herbs framed and hung as a collection create delicate yet graphic wall interest.

OPPOSITE: Low, wide wing chairs upholstered in a tawny wool tattersall suit casual meals and extended game play. An old apple-picking ladder echoes the rhythm of the French doors.

PREVIOUS SPREAD: The palette of the kitchen, from the pale olive green cabinetry to the soapstone counter and backsplash, and the stainless steel appliances and brushed nickel hardware, is a calm and cool counterpoint to the rough wooden post-and-beam framework, repeated in the central island. ABOVE: The window above the kitchen sink looks out to a shaded screened porch; its sill puts potted herbs right where they can be easily washed. RIGHT: A combination of wicker armchairs and wooden French bistro chairs surround the breakfast table, which is draped in an antique silk-embroidered textile from Tunisia.

ABOVE, LEFT: A collection of old pharmacy bottles gathered on a rustic wooden shelf
holds powders, bath salts, and an occasional branch or vine. Wrought-iron towel hooks
add permanent leaves. ABOVE, RIGHT: The powder room under the stairs is wrapped in
old heart-pine flooring and finished with compatible rustic accents like a garden pipe-
style tap, an iron lantern, and a tramp art mirror. OPPOSITE: Antique hobby horses put
their heads together in a bay window "corral" at the end of the entry balcony.

ABOVE: The beadboard tray ceiling in the master bedroom gives the space a lift and lends headroom for an iron canopy bed from PierceMartin. Grain-sack pillows and a heavy linen bedspread are perfectly casual bed dressings. An English trunk sitting atop a Turkish rug echoes the diamond motif of the Belgian armoire.
OPPOSITE: Rustic details like a twig planter and a wall-mounted lidded box, here used for brushes, suit a house by a lake. In the same vein, the bathtub taps are in a dull bronze finish and the roman shade is made of a soft linen.

OPPOSITE: The dado of boards painted cerulean encircles a guest bedroom. A sculptural birch chair and a hickory bed made locally bring the outdoors in, while a Romanian trunk, a table painted persimmon, and a "whistle" sign found at the flea market add fun color and folk flavor. ABOVE: Mirrors, some antique, some not, and all in frames with interesting profiles, cluster above an armless sofa. The stump drinks table has a cartoonish quality that offsets the industrial feel of the riveted table.

PREVIOUS SPREAD: The bunkroom offers four inviting and low-maintenance "nests" for younger guests. ABOVE: Classic hickory rockers line up to take in the view. OPPOSITE: Red Adirondack chairs beckon at the end of the dock.

TIMELESS BEAUTY

*S*tyles come and go, but I've always believed that truly good decorating supersedes trends, instead providing the perfect framework for an evolving life. Aside from the three D's (death, divorce, debt) that realtors credit for most of their business, there are, thankfully, more positive life changes, such as marriage, birth, and monetary comfort that also influence how we live. Through events big and small, we grow and change, with our tastes maturing along the way. Still, we all need good structure at the core.

I like to think that this house is a perfect example of an interior that feels fresh but will stand the test of time, the kind of home that will be as gracious and hospitable a generation from now as it was when it was built. The palette is neutral in a rich, handsome way; the furnishings have presence along with a feminine grace; the materials throughout are of the highest quality.

Architecturally, the plaster-coated walls and coved ceilings and gorgeous windows of French oak set a tone that is elegant and warm—two aspects that don't always appear in equal measure. Even empty, these rooms are beautiful. A lot of times as a designer you're working to disguise weaknesses. Not in this case.

Good architecture generates good decorating. When I am lucky enough to work with great spaces—rooms that are well-lit and beautifully proportioned, that flow smoothly one to the other—my mission is to make decorating decisions that will only lift them higher. It's a challenge and a thrill. Sometimes those decisions, as weighty as they may seem, come down to a question just this simple: What do you see when you enter a house, a room, a hallway? What sets a welcoming tone?

Whatever you see should be beautiful. Kim, an associate in my office, found the lacy iron candle sconces that hang from hooks in the front hall of this house. They're hardly the biggest or most dramatic object in the hall, but guests always notice them. They're unusual,

PREVIOUS PAGE: Bell jar lanterns, *demi-lune* tables, and a pair of French urns with scroll bases pick up on the soft curves established by the plastered barrel vault of the entry foyer. ABOVE: Lyrical furniture—a delicate French bench, a caned chair, an antique candlestick table and a standing lamp—accommodates impromptu performances near the piano in a bright end of the living room. OPPOSITE: At the fireplace end of the room, more substantial pieces like sofas in espresso mohair and a pair of high-backed Flemish chairs are balanced by an Italian trestle table with fanciful scrollwork, a filigree fire screen, and a wood and iron chandelier with decorative swags.

and because they are suspended, they have the slightest movement, so they seem alive. The eye naturally travels; you always want to provide interesting places for it to land.

Almost all the rooms in this house, except for the wood-paneled study and the deep gray/brown paneled dining room, have walls of cream and chalk gray, with the color integral to the plaster. The sweep of light walls could handle, even needed, the anchor of strong form. So in the living room nearly every piece of furniture has a distinct silhouette, each a composition of graceful curves, from the high-backed chairs to the chandelier to the piano. In a similar way, the dark wood hoops of the canopy bed in the master bedroom echo the curve of the coved ceiling. In this light-filled and spacious setting, the bed frame exhibits its stature proudly and creates a more intimate room within a room.

The further along I get in design, the more I value things that are special. I've always loved antiques, the true definition of "one-of-a-kind." Boxes in particular capture my fancy. An antique Regency box that was a Christmas gift from my mother years ago always finds pride of place wherever I live. At home on my bookcase I have a nascent collection of three nineteenth-century tortoiseshell boxes that were each a splurge. I'm just as happy with rustic boxes, especially when they're wearing a coat of beautiful cerulean-blue paint.

I'm always on the lookout for trunks and chests large in personality as well as size, because I think they're the perfect piece of furniture to place at the foot of a bed. I prefer a trunk to a bench, because you can both put things on it and tuck things in it. Against the open framework of a bed, a trunk provides a solid counterweight. It's also a great spot for visitors to rest their luggage, and every guest loves a host who anticipates his or her needs.

Textiles, like antiques, are a surefire and relatively affordable way to lend character to an interior. Much as I like checks and plaids, I'm not a huge fan of other patterned fabrics. But I'll seize any opportunity to use an antique textile, such as a section of tapestry. Rebecca Vizard makes custom pillows incorporating exquisite fabrics and trims. Her pillows saved the deep velvet sofas in this living room from melting into pools of dark chocolate. I also love a monogram. For the high-backed chairs in the dining room, a monogram added just the right decorative and personal flourish.

LEFT: Randomly mixing chairs upholstered in tapestry with those done up in ivory
wool crowned by a monogram tempers tradition in an otherwise formal dining room.
FOLLOWING SPREAD: His and her club chairs and a pair of desk chairs plumped
with blue velvet cushions suit the use of the study off the master bedroom.

EVERYTHING IN ITS PLACE

Whether you live with many things or few, putting them in order matters. Neatness is a religion for some, so it follows that the epigram "a place for everything and everything in its place" originated with the Reverend Charles Augustus Goodrich. The message is true, and following it simply makes life not only easier but lovelier. You (and everyone else in the family) know where to find what you're looking for, and where to put it back when you've finished with it. Special places to store things, from antique cupboards and custom cabinets, provide extra incentive.

◆ Step one is to take stock of what you have and what matters to you and make proper space for it. If it's shoes (who doesn't love shoes?), then organize them in a user-friendly manner. As a daily activity, isn't scanning neat shelves or racks for the pair you wish to wear far preferable to rummaging around in the bottom of a closet?

◆ Closets can be tucked away between rooms, but they can also be treated as furniture. In this house, in the hallway linking the master bedroom and bathroom, two pairs of beautiful wood doors form armoire-like storage closets flanking a window.

◆ Men and women have such different needs when it comes to personal care, why should they be treated uniformly? In the master bathroom of this house, she has a sit-down vanity adjacent to the sink; he has a shaving mirror and window in the shower.

◆ Kitchens demand more organizational work than any other room in the house. And more storage. But you don't want the kitchen to be a sea of nothing but cabinetry. I like to balance ample and well-detailed cupboards and drawers with a variety of open shelves. Bring pretty things you use out into the light. This house has a wonderful blend of open and closed storage, primary and secondary kitchen spaces, pantries, and even a special room for silver.

◆ Barring space constraints, make your laundry area a pleasant place to be. We wouldn't want to treat our bathrooms as afterthoughts. Why do so with laundry rooms? Wide counters and plenty of storage go beyond merely being useful for laundry; they also serve well as gift-wrapping and craft areas.

PREVIOUS SPREAD: Elegant proportions rule in the kitchen, though the materials shift from more refined for the painted island to more rustic for the antique oak cupboards on the periphery. RIGHT: With its plaster box form and wood trim that matches the cabinetry, the stove hood reads as an integral architectural element.

ABOVE: In a secondary prep area, Italian marble cladding behind the open shelves elevates their contents, mostly oversize serving pieces that suit the scale of the shelving. OPPOSITE: A laundry room off a back hall is as thoroughly and thoughtfully outfitted as the kitchen. FOLLOWING SPREAD: Seating in chenille, suede, and wool plaid, and plentiful wood surfaces, make the sunny family room the easy-care, comfortable room it should be.

PREVIOUS SPREAD: For a son's bedroom, deep chocolate linen curtains, a chair and ottoman in charcoal velvet, a reclaimed fir bed, and an antique trunk with leather detailing project a refined, masculine look. ABOVE: Architectural iron fragments were converted to bedside lamps. OPPOSITE: As in the adjoining bedroom, the bathroom curtains were embroidered with a custom cream leaf motif on their leading and bottom edges. The rounded edges of the antique oak sink base complement the similar treatment of the plaster tub enclosure.

PREVIOUS SPREAD: Bedrooms for a son (LEFT) and daughter (RIGHT) each feature a distinctive bedframe, cabriole-leg bedside tables, spindle lamps, simple linen curtains, and antique rugs atop nearly wall-to-wall sisal. ABOVE: The tub in the master bath sits in its own vaulted chapel-like space, lit by a leaded glass oculus and at night by beaded sconces. OPPOSITE: An ivory linen stool tucks under a Bardiglio marble counter that accommodates her sink and vanity; his sink is in the niche beyond, as is the shower.

ABOVE: White cushions, overscale pots, and limestone paving, along with boxwood hedges, make the pool area an elegant outdoor room. OPPOSITE: The combination of temperate weather and an outdoor fireplace means the terrace is used nearly year-round and furnished accordingly with substantial stone tables and iron chairs with thick cushions.

A GLAMOROUS THREAD

*U*nless you are a total historicist or a complete modernist, putting a house together in the twenty-first century involves navigating both the old and the new. Either you have an older home that needs to be reconfigured for contemporary life, or you have a new home that would benefit from the gravitas of age, something good decorating can provide. To me, decorating should occupy a pedestal as elevated as architecture, because it makes enormous contributions to developing character in a space. Decoration is what turns a house into a home.

A new modern house, especially if it is furnished exclusively with contemporary pieces, runs the risk of looking like a showroom. In order to come alive, it needs a depth that comes from layering, a variety of materials, and thoughtful detailing. Even if you are starting from scratch, with no personal collections of art or objects to incorporate, your house will benefit enormously from a personal point of view. French modernism guided the design for this house, lending an Atlanta home Gallic sophistication and savoir faire.

I have interior designer Charles Gandy (a talented professional for whom I worked and whom I much admire) to thank for introducing me to the work of legendary French designer Jean-Michel Frank. From a paneled wall to a marquetry sideboard to a simple footed bowl, Frank combined clean lines and a subtle palette with luxurious materials in a way that gives his interiors a lightness of being. As stylized and stylish as his work was, it was also calm, inviting, and comfortable, French without the hauteur, which, to me, provided the perfect direction for an elegant house, American-style.

A Frank interior considered every surface, not just the things that populate a room. There's a tendency to think that modern spaces need little in the way of architectural detailing, but in fact things like doors and doorframes, mantels and moldings are all the more noticeable in a lean interior. It was as if the late Jean-Michel himself were looking over my shoulder when I designed details to complement the lofty spaces with architects Keith Summerour and Greg Nott.

The profile of the stepped baseboards may be sharp and severe, but the simple act of adding molding warms the rooms, because it references human scale. Niches, ribbed doorframes, limestone fluted columns in the living room's double-height space, and a mantelpiece with ribbed pilasters had the same effect. The design details are all straight lines, but their three-dimensional form captures light and shadow. Using limestone—a classic French building material prized for its warmth and evenness of tone—and Venetian plaster also softened the hard edges and geometric forms.

One whole wall of the living room is composed of windows, so light absolutely floods in. Big windows are another common trope in new houses. If you're not going to fight the light by blocking it out—and why would you, unless the view is horrific or the room is mostly a nighttime space—then you need to balance it. Otherwise, the eye is constantly struggling to shift between light and dark. It's uncomfortable to be in a room that feels like a cave into which someone is shining a searchlight. You want the light to embrace you from all sides.

In keeping with the monochromatic color scheme, limestone floors and walls painted a similar tone ensure that one surface is not more important than the other. Two Tibetan rugs in sister patterns and the same hue create intimate seating islands in the large room. Jean-Michel Frank sofas and club chairs, timeless in their form and comfort, practically meld into the rugs; the similarity in color helps reduce their bulk.

The darkest elements in this room are on the small side: end tables, drinks tables, the coffee table, and some accessories. The one exception is the painting above the fireplace, because it needed to add weight to the vast expanse of wall. With one last nod to Frank and French elegance, touches of gold alight in the room in chairs with gilded arms and feet and pillow fabrics with metallic threads.

PREVIOUS SPREAD: In the long and lofty living room, everything needed to be scaled up a bit: lamps are taller, sofas are larger, even the logs in the fireplace are longer. OPPOSITE: The curves of a Chinese-inspired coffee table, a three-legged iron drinks table, and the gilded frames of fireplace chairs offset the square forms of the Jean-Michel Frank–inspired club chairs and sofa. FOLLOWING SPREAD: With elegant details like a high back and waterfall skirt, a custom sofa in the study balances the fireplace opposite it. Klismos chairs offer a place to cozy up to the fire.

GEOMETRIC AND ORGANIC: THE RIGHT BALANCE

I have always believed that setting off one motif by contrasting it with another makes both shine more brightly. Think of how much more dynamic a checkerboard becomes when you add the round game pieces to the grid.

◆ When a room has a lot of rectilinear features, whether architectural or decorative, I choose to soften it with more organic shapes. The foyer of this house is dominated by squares—the front door window panels, the coffered ceiling, the design of the rug. To balance them, I installed sconces, side chairs, and a console table that all feature sinuous lines. The iron base of the table has the elegance and flourish of elaborate penmanship.

◆ Much as I love the linear designs and geometric forms associated with Jean-Michel Frank, I like to throw a curve or two into the mix. In the living room of this house, the gentle contours of the coffee table, lamps, fireside chairs, and drinks tables invite the eye and body to navigate more gracefully around the boxier shapes of the sofas and club chairs.

◆ Geometric usually reads as hard, organic as soft. Both come together around the dining table in this house. Like gold braiding on an officer's uniform, gold-leafed chairs with Greek key arms contribute a bright line amid more somber solids. A mix of seating also saves a dining room with a large table from feeling like a conference room.

◆ A blend of materials is just as essential as a balance of forms. A room dominated by hard-edged contemporary furniture, for instance, needs the relief of something soft, like an ottoman upholstered in plush mohair. No matter how chic a room looks, it only succeeds if it puts people at ease.

OPPOSITE: The arms of the Murano chandelier over the dining table pick up the curves of the iron base of the console in the entry hall and the sconces above it.

PREVIOUS SPREAD: Venetian plaster walls in rich chocolate and floor-to-ceiling curtains of wool sateen warm the dining room, as do eight chairs upholstered in eggplant damask. Gold-framed Greek key chairs contribute a bright linear note. Though contemporary, the walnut buffet cabinet and dining table have a distinctly art deco feel. RIGHT: A one-armed sofa, lavender and Lucite, dress down and perk up the breakfast room.

193

RIGHT: The double canopy rails of the custom matte-black-lacquer bed reference the deep boxy pelmets of the window treatments. A chaise in light taupe mohair and two chairs in pale blue velvet form a cozy sitting area at the foot of the bed.

MODERN FAMILY

As with any involved creative project, decorating is a ride that swings from exhilarating to challenging and back again. For some people, picking out colors and fabrics is a thrill; for others it's overwhelming. And that's just the "fun" stuff. Decorating a house is a collaborative endeavor. Even if you're doing it yourself, there will be makers and doers helping you realize your vision.

If you hire a designer, she or he will be captain of a team and of a process with many moving parts. Though in most people's minds the designer or decorator enters a project as the architect exits (at least with new construction), in the best of all possible worlds decoration and architecture develop simultaneously. Such was the case with this house on which I worked with architect Keith Summerour. The more fluent the dialogue, the better the outcome.

Take, for instance, the lighting plan for the magnificent stair rotunda of this Atlanta house. Inspired by Thomas Jefferson's designs for the University of Virginia campus, the rotunda is formal and classical, but it also has a lyrical simplicity that makes it a graceful focal point at the center of the house. Though it is lit at the top by oculus windows, the stair winds through three floors, requiring no fewer than twenty-eight sconces along the way. To determine the positioning of the electrical boxes for the sconces, I had to wait until the stairs were installed so that I could climb them and intuitively feel where the lighting should go.

Decorating is a hands-on business. Experience guides the professional, but even for me, nothing beats being in the space to sense the perfect color, the right proportion, or the ideal placement. Being involved early on allowed me to make all kinds of adjustments in this

house. In the master bath, there is a pocket for the electronic solar shades to tuck into. The counter at the bar near the screening room is higher than usual to hide any mess. The lofty kitchen has niches within an alcove specifically designed to house the range and fridge.

Above all, this is a family house with an arrangement of space that accommodates modern life. To the right of the entry hall is an intimate suite of rooms—a cypress-lined study and office and the master bedroom and bath. To the left is a series of spacious open areas that flow gracefully from one to the other—eating area to kitchen to family room right on out to a covered seating area centered on a fireplace. Gone is the formal living room.

Since the suite is for grownups, I furnished it accordingly, with upright wing chairs upholstered in crewelwork, English walnut tables with turned legs, and antique leather chairs that are my go-to for an instant and impactful dose of character, patina, and style. In the family room, everything is lower, wider, and more cushion-y, signaling a relaxed space for all ages.

Bridging the two is an octagonal dining room, the final vestige of a more formal way of living brought into a less formal time. Though traditional in arrangement, with high-backed chairs surrounding an enormous table over which hangs a large chandelier, this room steers clear of the stiff and staid that speed too many dining rooms to Siberia.

This room is on a path that leads into the garden. The image in my head was of an elegant picnic staged in a deep cool glade. I wanted it to feel as if nature herself had been my collaborator. The custom octagonal carpet is like a bed of sun-bleached pine needles. The walls, trim, doors, and window frames are all the same shade (albeit in a different finish) of forest green with a touch of olive, as are the curtains. The flower arrangement mixes lighter greens in a faux bois cement planter. Chairs upholstered in a rich yet friendly tapestry fabric provide the only pattern, one of leaves and branches.

Rather than adhering to an outmoded plan, this house acknowledges how much times have changed. I wanted the decorating to follow suit.

PREVIOUS PAGE: Twenty-eight sconces and gold leaf–framed antique herbiers line the stair that climbs the central skylit rotunda. The handcrafted iron stair rail is the work of Atlantan Charles Calhoun. OPPOSITE: Painted a deep warm green, with wool curtains in the same tone, the octagonal dining room is an elegant extension of the garden. At night, the generous round table surrounded by tapestry-upholstered Canterbury chairs is lit exclusively by a graceful wood and iron chandelier. The mirror over the antique Italian buffet doubles the sparkle.

OPPOSITE: An antique Oushak carpet, its warm tones in tune with the limestone fireplace surround, brightens the cypress-paneled study. The height of the central seventeenth-century Italian table, higher than a coffee table, is a gracious platform for serving refreshments. *Botany Bay Plantation Marsh Road*, a painting by John Folsom, creates a window into a languid Southern landscape. ABOVE: An antique carved handkerchief table serves a pair of wing chairs upholstered in linen crewelwork fabric, each outfitted with a striped velvet pillow.

CURTAINS:
WORTH ALL DUE RESPECT

Curtains can be taken for granted. Of course we need them; they protect us from the sun, the cold, and prying eyes. But, in addition to their primary function, they are the ultimate accessory. Imagine a room without them and it practically collapses, because they are as essential to decoration as structural columns are to architecture.

◆ Curtains are the ultimate softies. They visually soften the walls of a room, soften daylight by filtering it, and soften noise by absorbing it. Given such a workload, they need fuel in the form of plenty of yardage, at minimum two times the width of a window. There's nothing sadder than a skimpy curtain and nothing prettier than a full one that drapes beautifully.

◆ Almost every curtain at the big and beautiful windows in this house falls from ceiling to floor on a simple iron rod. It's my favorite way to handle window treatments, because they contribute so much to the structure of a room. Since they're often the most dominant vertical element, I want to emphasize their length above

all. For curtain material, nothing beats wool; it hangs well and doesn't wrinkle.

◆ Even when a room doesn't need blackout conditions for sleeping or movie viewing, it's nice to have a sheer curtain to provide an extra layer of visual security and of decoration. The study in this house features tall corner windows that look out on a lovely garden. During the day, the lightweight wool curtains in a subtle plaid are usually open. Sometimes they are pulled shut to temper the brightness for someone working at the computer. At night, when closed, they transform walls of dark glass into pale screens of soft ripples.

◆ Curtains in a bathroom feel especially luxurious because, other than towels, they provide the only soft surface in a room of shiny, hard materials. Though this bathroom has roman shades that pull up into built-in valances above the windowed doors to the outside, curtains seemed more appropriate for the alcove the tub sits in. They add a note of voluptuousness in tune with a luxurious soak.

OPPOSITE: Burnished leather chairs from Robuck and Co., a desk and table with turned legs, and scroll ironwork sconces lend the office style and character along with function. The diamond-patterned sisal rug, nearly wall-to-wall, brings the antiques into the twenty-first century.

PREVIOUS SPREAD: The depth and breadth of the kitchen reflect its prominent role in the family. Housed within the alcove framed by an arch are the range, refrigerator, freezer, fryer, steamer, and pantry. Custom iron pendants with pleated linen shades light the islands. ABOVE: Upper cabinets are a combination of solid wooden doors and framed glass doors with lead muntins. OPPOSITE: In the breakfast room, a Henri II bench and low-back side chairs, all upholstered in a brown and tan checked linen, pull up to a refectory table.

PREVIOUS PAGES, LEFT: In the family room, James McLaughlin Way's *Black Horse* glows above an English roll-arm sofa upholstered in a dark chocolate chenille. PREVIOUS PAGES, RIGHT: That comfort is king is demonstrated by two sofas and a pair of club chairs on swivel bases, all generous in size, surrounding an antique English table modified to put-up-your-feet height. ABOVE: The octagonal dining room lines up with the center of the pool, with master suite to the left and family area to the right. OPPOSITE: By the outdoor fireplace, resin wicker sofas are dressed in cushions of light stone outdoor fabric with a contrasting brown welt; a chair and an ottoman are in brown and ivory stripes.

ABOVE: A simple curtain framing the window by the tub and roman shades over the doors leading to the garden, both in gray and ivory pinstriped fabric, provide softness and privacy in the master bath. A bronze bell lantern and an overscaled ottoman upholstered in ivory terry cloth anchor the center of the room. OPPOSITE: The linear forms of an American iron chandelier, strapwork canopy, and curtain rod embellish the clean barrel-vaulted space of the master bedroom. Placed by the window, a pair of Louis XIII fireside wing chairs provide a charming spot to read.

ABOVE: The color red cheers a young girl's bedroom in the form of two painted wicker bedside tables, a sleigh bed upholstered in cream and red plaid, a pair of slipper chairs in red linen, and patchwork-patterned curtains accented with red ties. Little hand-carved birds perch sweetly on the branches of an iron floor lamp. OPPOSITE: The same fabric appears in roman shades in the en-suite bathroom with its bright red vanity. Brackets at two corners of the Botticino marble counter provide shelves for favorite objects.

RIGHT: Between the garage and the kitchen is the room every family dreams of: a practical place to work on all sorts of projects. A desk dropped down from the counter running below the windows is set up for both home office and homework. Cupboards with diamond-shaped cutouts in their doors give every family member a locker for outerwear and sports equipment. Drawers, cabinets, and baskets organize materials for crafts, gift-wrapping, art, sewing, and school projects, while a central counter furnished with stools provides a work surface generous enough to accommodate all endeavors.

COMING HOME

*I*t makes sense that my most recent house should be the oldest I have lived in as an adult. How many of us circle back, consciously or not, to the places that made the deepest imprints on our young senses? For me, that would be the farmhouse my grandparents lived in for sixty years. Its white clapboard exterior capped by a red metal roof was as pure country as the sweetly scented hay bales we kids used to help unload on our weekly visits to the farm.

Such houses are rare in Atlanta, due to the Civil War fire that destroyed much of the city, but I have the good fortune to live in an unusually charming, decidedly Mayberry-ish historic neighborhood. Whittier Mill Village was an early progressive community that grew up around a textile mill along the Chattahoochee River. My house was built in 1897, likely as a duplex to better accommodate the many mill workers. It has a wide front porch, a deep hip roof, and a screened door through which my orange tabby cat, Okie, keeps an eye on things.

I moved to this house from a loft I had created in the original village general store only a few blocks away. I was already craving more space when life stepped in and pretty much demanded it; two years ago, I married a man with three sons. My house is not big, but in the move from my loft I did gain—in addition to three wonderful stepsons—an upstairs, a welcoming front yard, and a back yard that is bordered on two sides by the Whittier Mill Park.

My love for simple farmhouses rises in the presence of heart pine floors and beadboard wainscoting, but falls in the absence of closets and cupboards and pantries. I cannot live an ordered life without storage. Not unlike a boat, every inch of this house had to work hard, so I gained space and imposed order by reconfiguring closets, reorienting bathrooms, and borrowing back neglected space under the eaves.

I have always loved spatial problem-solving as much as decorating. Just because a house is historic doesn't mean you can't make modifications that suit modern life. Updates and improvements carried out in a clever and subtle manner come across as thoughtful

restoration. When a house's plan and details make sense, it seems as if they have always been that way: the house becomes its better self.

In an older house, storage is always a major issue. These days, we may be able to replace shelves of photo albums with a single memory stick, but rare is the person who can live without stuff. I'll be the first to admit that things have meaning to me—sometimes for pure sentiment, sometimes simply for beauty—and I love being surrounded by them.

My new house is filled with favorite pieces from past homes that I always make room for. In the living room, the sofa is flanked by an old Swedish table with quirky asymmetrical drawers and a French wine-tasting table. I love having generous tabletops within reach of a sofa. They can handle stacks of books, vases of flowers, and large lamps that contribute a vertical element to the composition of a room.

An old leather wing chair beloved by my cats—as evidenced by their scratchy contributions to its patina—is now my husband Kevinn's favorite perch in the living room. My father is ever-present in an antique Italian footstool that I recently reupholstered. Whenever he visited me in my old place, the stool was the boost he needed to climb up into the very high bed in my guest bedroom.

I have long collected black and white photographs, all of which made the move. I love my Todd Murphy print of a gauzy baby dress, a ghostlike image that is, for me, as modern as it is sentimental. And I've always been fond of a New York City street scene by Elliott Erwitt because the woman depicted gazing up at the Empire State Building reminds me of my mother as she looks in photos from the 1950s. They both have the same tiny waist and curly black hair.

I'm so used to having a deadline for outfitting a house that I appreciate the luxury of time that comes with collecting for myself. Finding just the right piece requires patience (and a placeholder until it shows up), but the satisfaction is deepened by the wait.

Such was the case with the Dutch armoire that proudly fills the niche to the left of the fireplace in my living room. It's one of my newest acquisitions, yet one of my most treasured. I love its simple form and graphic black molding, as well as the fact that it hides the television. It's useful and practical and elegant without being fancy. Which for a country house in the city is something I would call the perfect combination.

PAGE 217: The big and little drawers in an old Swedish table make it a favorite piece of furniture that has followed me everywhere. A Philip Moulthrop vessel and an antique banded box satisfy my love of warm wood tones. PREVIOUS SPREAD: The living room brings together elegant and hardworking materials I turn to over and over: mohair (on the sofa), leather, tapestry, linen, rush matting, iron, and wood. I found the African stool (tucked under the French wine-tasting table) on a trip to Malawi and flew home with it on my lap. Lamps made of iron architectural fragments lend the room a vertical element and a change in scale. OPPOSITE: Michael Dines' painting takes pride of place above an original fireplace I sheathed in beadboard from hearth to ceiling.

PREVIOUS SPREAD: Glass-fronted French cupboards from an old bakery now house a collection of Haviland china from my great-aunt Mabel as well as serving pieces my mother adds to every year. Next to the window, concrete planters by a folk artist from the Southwest sit atop a pair of mismatched artists' stools. OPPOSITE: An Italian chandelier adds the sparkle I love in a dining room. ABOVE, LEFT: Simple foliate candle sconces flank a gilded American mirror, c. 1880, that is a little older than the house. ABOVE, RIGHT: Lamp shades made of porcupine quills draw the eye to black-and-white photographs from my collection.

MAKING COUNTRY CHIC

"Country" is the look Americans are most at home with. I love farmhouse tables and hooked rugs and old signs as much as the next person, but a house filled with nothing but rusticity starts to feel less like a home than a set for *Little House on the Prairie*. A house should reflect the times we live in as much as a past we revere. Just as with any period or style, it's about balance. Any heritage is best celebrated visually when it is embraced selectively.

◆ Adapting antiques is an easy way to bring something old into our time. The scale and linear form of the rusty ironwork bases of a pair of lamps in my living room already lend them a modern air. Topping them with brown linen shades made them thoroughly contemporary. The antique leather sofa in my study originally had three lumpy leather seat cushions. Replacing them with a single mohair cushion made the sofa more modern, more interesting, and definitely more comfortable.

◆ Rustic finishes need contrast to shine. The Swedish armoire in my bedroom has long been a favorite of mine for its contours and glorious blue color. Atop it sits a big basket once used for bringing piglets to market. The warm and wonderful character of both is set off by the crisp white and gray walls of the room.

◆ An old technique can be used in a modern way to great effect. I've always loved spatterware for its friendly liveliness. It was my inspiration for turning a low and dark bedroom under the eaves into a bright and happy room. The spatter effect softened all the angles and created a lighthearted canopy that's almost the reverse of a starry night. Replacing a small window with one much larger and more interesting also lit up the space.

PREVIOUS SPREAD: For the old leather sofa in the study I had a single mohair cushion made to replace three lumpy original ones. I love the mustard color of the old American cabinet and the huge scale of the lantern that hangs overhead. Its sister hovers over my office conference table.
OPPOSITE: The animals and landscape I grew up with are never far from me. In the study, a weathered carousel horse strides beneath a photographic painting of a country road by John Folsom.

ABOVE: The footprint of my bedroom is tight but the ceilings are high, so I went tall with a canopy bed and installed reading lights on the wall. In rearranging some space to carve out a master bath I saved the transom window marked "510." OPPOSITE: A Swedish armoire with a wonderful faded blue finish was a coat closet in my former residence; now it holds my dresses. Atop it sits a basket for carrying piglets to market. The wheeled trunk at the foot of the bed holds my gift-wrapping supplies.

ABOVE: For years I used the white iron stool, now beneath the vintage double sink in the upstairs bath, as a drafting stool. It originally belonged to my grandfather, an orthopedic surgeon. I bought the sink three years ago and stored it in the crawlspace under the house until I was ready to install it. I love how the gilded mirrors dress it up. OPPOSITE: One of my oldest pieces, a Swedish carved armoire, sits in the hall between the dining room and my bedroom and stores hats and gloves. FOLLOWING SPREAD: Replacing a small window with an elegant arched one opened up a bedroom under the eaves. I designed a speckled paint finish reminiscent of spatterware, which was executed to perfection by artist Jill Biskin. The wall finish adds a lighthearted spirit to, and softens the angles of, a room used by my stepsons.

ACKNOWLEDGMENTS

I like to walk through my neighborhood in the morning with the sunlight streaming through the trees. While I walk, I pray, think, plan, pant, design, and dream. I daydream a lot during those morning walks, but I never dreamt about a book until I was introduced to the one and only, Jill Cohen. With her encouragement and guidance, I started the process of creating a book. She introduced me to the brilliant writer, Heather MacIsaac, who makes me sound more interesting than I actually am; to the talented creative team of Doug Turshen and Steve Turner who produced a beautiful, elegant layout; and to the patient Kathleen Jayes at Rizzoli who helped guide all of our efforts.

During this process, I have been overwhelmed with gratitude to those who have influenced me, guided me, supported me, hired me, and embraced me throughout my career. To the many artisans and fabricators, clients and architects, builders and subcontractors, and showrooms and installers, I cannot imagine even attempting to design and decorate without you. So much of writing a book involves reflection and so many names have come to mind. I offer my most sincere thank you to Bobby Garrett, Ken Berry, Keith Summerour, Yong Pak, Charles Heydt, Greg Nott, Brad Heppner, Norman Askins, Brad Wright, Erica and Michael Dines, Charles Calhoun, Linda and Gil Horsley, Ryan Hughes, Judy Pratt, Craig Swenson, Clinton Smith, Shane Robuck, Kristen Marooney, Hal Ainsworth, Winton Noah, Tim and Bill Sullivan, Robert Hampton, Dan Cahoon, Courtney and Randy Tilinski, Barbara Brown, Greg Crawford, Brian Bleshoy, Richard Ross, Charles Gandy, Bill Peace, Nancy Braithwaite, Amy Morris, John Westbrook, Terri Herzog-Navas, Ann Rast, and Junior. Special thanks to the clients who gave me my first big projects, Beth Belanger and Carol Farbolin. Without those gracious clients allowing me to disrupt their lives and photograph their homes, there would be no book to publish. So, thank you!

When you sit in a room together every day for over a decade, you cannot help but become way too involved in each other's lives. And so it has happened to "the girls" and I. The girls, Kim Winkler and Elizabeth Hanson, are two of the most talented designers I know and I am blessed to have them working with me every day. Rounding out "Team Westbrook" (as they like to say) is Laurie Stephens, who brings youth into the office, and Kathy Wedbush, with her great style and humor. Thank you!

My dear husband, Kevinn, continues to be my head cheerleader. He and his three redheaded sons have brought much joy and laughter into my life. My brother, Stephen, his wife, Delisa, and their four gorgeous children—Paul, Daniel, Michael, and Jana, plus Henry, the dog with apricot ears—have been a steadfast support system and a needed distraction from my obsession with design. Thank you!

From the time I was a little girl, my parents encouraged my artistic side. Through their example, they have shown me what service, faith, and unconditional love look like. Jeremiah 29:11-14. I love you, Mom and Dad. Thank you! Thank you! Thank you!

CREDITS

Endpapers by Michael Dines

Calligraphy by Katy Burge

PHOTOGRAPHY BY PAGE NUMBER:
Erica George Dines: 2-4, 6, 11, 37-39, 41-55, 57-68, 71, 73-89, 91, 113-119, 121-123, 125-134, 137, 141-143, 146-148, 150, 152-155, 157-160, 162-165, 167-181, 197, 199-201, 203-217, 219-221, 223-229, 231-237

Pieter Estersohn: 13, 15-27, 29-35, 183, 185-187, 189-195

Quentin Bacon: 138, 139, 144, 145, 146, 149, 151

William Waldron: 92, 93, 95-99, 101-111

ARCHITECTS AND BUILDERS
The Lightness of Being
Architect: Keith Summerour, Summerour & Associates
Builder: Craig Carver, The Carver Group

For the Generations
Architect: Brad Wright, Wright Design
Builder: Ken Berry, The Berry Group

Grand with Grace
Architect: Yong Pak & Charles Heydt,
Pak Heydt & Associates

Dressing Up, Dressing Down
Builder: Nick Breiding, Breiding Construction

Ode to a View
Architect: Keith Summerour, Summerour & Associates

Timeless Beauty
Architect: Keith Summerour, Summerour & Associates
Builder: Ken Berry, The Berry Group

A Glamorous Thread
Architect: Keith Summerour, Summerour & Associates
Builder: Joe Noah, Noah & Associates

Modern Family
Architect: Keith Summerour, Summerour & Associates
Builder: Rick Fierer, Bildon Construction

Coming Home
Builder (1st Phase): Chad Kohls
Builder (2nd Phase): Nick Breiding/ Breiding Construction

First published in the United States of America in 2015
by Rizzoli International Publications, Inc.
300 Park Avenue South
New York, NY 10010
www.rizzoliusa.com

© 2015 Barbara Westbrook

2015 2016 2017 2018 / 10 9 8 7 6 5 4 3 2 1

Distributed in the U.S. trade by Random House, New York

Printed in China

ISBN-13: 978-0-8478-4505-7

Library of Congress Catalog Control Number: 2014949599

Design by Doug Turshen with Steve Turner